HÄGAR
THE HORRIBLE

BY
DIK BROWNE

ANiMAL
HAUS!

JOVE BOOKS, NEW YORK

HÄGAR THE HORRIBLE: ANIMAL HAUS!

A Jove Book / published by arrangement with
King Features Syndicate, Inc.

PRINTING HISTORY
Tempo edition / 1981
Charter edition / April 1987
Jove edition / May 1990

ISBN: 0-515-10327-6

Jove Books are published by The Berkley Publishing Group,
200 Madison Avenue, New York, New York 10016.
The name "JOVE" and the "J" logo
are trademarks belonging to Jove Publications, Inc.

PRINTED IN THE UNITED STATES OF AMERICA

10 9 8 7 6 5 4 3 2 1

3-4 DIK BROWNE

5-23 DIK BROWNE

6-5 DIK BROWNE

6-17 DIK BROWNE

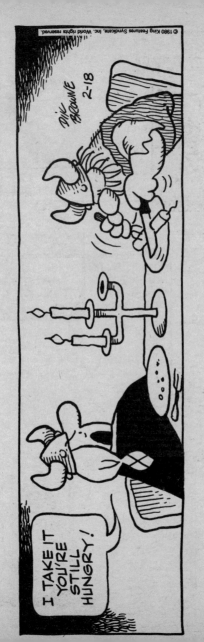